THE 5-DAY WEALTH PLAN

The 5-Day Wealth Plan

Build Your Financial Freedom

B. Vincent

QuillQuest Publishers

CONTENTS

INTRODUCTION

Embracing Independence from the rat race

In reality as we know it where monetary vulnerability appears to linger at each corner, the journey for independence from the rat race has become more important than any other time in recent memory. Independence from the rat race — frequently imagined as a far off dream including perpetual riches and relaxation — is, as a general rule, about overseeing one's monetary predetermination. It's tied in with bringing in your cash work for you, as opposed to being subjugated by the consistent pattern of procuring and spending. Yet, how can one explore the perplexing ways of ventures, investment funds, and spending plans to accomplish this sought after state? The response lies in a purposeful, very much organized approach: an abundance plan.

The Significance of an Abundance Plan

An abundance plan isn't simply a bunch of monetary techniques; it's a guide that guides you from your ongoing monetary circumstance to your definitive objective of independence from the rat race. It incorporates grasping your monetary wellbeing, defining reachable objectives, settling on informed choices, and changing your course as life unfurls. Without an arrangement, dealing with your funds can want to cruise without a compass — aimless and inclined to becoming mixed up in the blustery oceans of monetary vulnerability.

Presenting The 5-Day Abundance Plan

The "5-Day Abundance Plan" is intended to be your compass in the journey for independence from the rat race. This plan distils complex monetary ideas into pragmatic, step by step activities that can be executed by anybody, no matter what their monetary proficiency or beginning stage. Throughout five days, you will set out on an excursion to:

Evaluate Your Monetary Wellbeing: Understanding where you stand monetarily is the underpinning of any abundance plan. On Day 1, you'll figure out how to assess what is happening, making way for the days to follow.

Plan and Financial plan: With an unmistakable comprehension of your monetary wellbeing, Day 2 spotlights on making a spending plan and investment funds system that lines up with your monetary objectives, preparing for maintainable abundance gathering.

Contribute for What's to come: Day 3 demystifies the universe of effective financial planning, directing you through the essentials of making a broadened venture portfolio to develop your abundance after some time.

Safeguard Your Abundance: On Day 4, you'll investigate how to shield your monetary accomplishments through protection, lawful insurances, and other gamble the executives systems.

Make a Practical Abundance Plan: At last, Day 5 is tied in with uniting everything into a strong, adaptable abundance plan that can develop with your changing requirements and objectives, guaranteeing long haul independence from the rat race.

The Excursion Ahead

Setting out on "The 5-Day Abundance Plan" is something beyond perusing a book; it's tied in with making proactive strides towards a more brilliant, safer monetary future. Every day of the arrangement is intended to be noteworthy, furnishing you with the information and devices you want to fabricate a strong starting point for your independence from the rat race. Toward the finish of these five days, you'll not just have a more clear comprehension of your monetary scene yet in addition a customized guide to direct your monetary choices pushing ahead.

Allow this excursion to be the defining moment in your monetary life. As you flip through the pages of this book, recollect that each section is a bit nearer to accomplishing the independence from the rat race you've generally longed for. The way to abundance is reachable, and everything begins with an arrangement. Welcome to the 5-Day Abundance Plan.

1

DAY 1: ASSESSING YOUR FINANCIAL HEALTH

Prologue to Monetary Wellbeing

Welcome to Day 1 of your excursion toward independence from the rat race. Today, we center around a basic initial step: surveying your monetary wellbeing. Understanding where you stand monetarily is likened to diagnosing your actual wellbeing prior to settling on a tight eating routine or exercise plan. It gives an unmistakable image of your beginning stage, featuring qualities to expand upon and difficulties to address.

Figuring out Your Ongoing Position

Total assets: Your Monetary Preview

Definition: Your total assets is the absolute worth of your resources short your liabilities. Resources

4

incorporate money, ventures, property, and whatever else of worth you own. Liabilities are your obligations, including advances, contracts, and some other cash you owe.

The most effective method to Ascertain: Rundown every one of your resources and their qualities, then list every one of your liabilities and their sums. Take away the all out liabilities from the complete resources for view as your total assets.

Significance: Knowing your total assets provides you with a depiction of your monetary wellbeing and is a urgent beginning stage for arranging.

Pay versus Costs: The Progression of Your Funds

Pay Sources: Index all types of revenue, including compensations, rewards, ventures, and any side gigs.

Following Costs: Record every month to month cost, arranging them into basics (lodging, food, utilities) and trivial items (feasting out, diversion).

Balance Examination: Contrast your absolute pay with your complete costs to check whether you're living inside your means or spending more than you acquire.

Obligation Evaluation: Grasping Your Liabilities

Kinds of Obligation: Distinguish all obligations, including Visa obligation, understudy loans, vehicle advances, and home loans.

Loan fees and Terms: Note the financing cost and reimbursement terms for every obligation to focus on which ones to take care of first.

Relationship of debt to salary after taxes: Work out your relationship of debt to salary after taxes by partitioning your complete month to month obligation installments by your gross month to month pay. This proportion evaluates your obligation level and monetary wellbeing.

Laying out Monetary Objectives

With a reasonable comprehension of your monetary wellbeing, now is the ideal time to define practical monetary objectives. These can go from momentary targets like putting something aside for a get-away to long haul objectives like retirement investment funds. Guarantee your objectives are Explicit, Quantifiable, Reachable, Pertinent, and Time-bound (Brilliant).

Activity Steps for Day 1

Ascertain Your Total assets: Utilize the technique illustrated above to decide your ongoing total assets.

Dissect Your Pay and Costs: Make a nitty gritty rundown of your pay sources and month to month costs to figure out your monetary stream.

Survey Your Obligation: Rundown every one of your obligations, noticing the financing costs and terms, to focus on reimbursement procedures.

Put forth Monetary Objectives: In light of your monetary evaluation, put forth Shrewd monetary objectives that you mean to accomplish.

Day 1 of the 5-Day Abundance Plan is tied in with understanding where you stand monetarily. By investigating your total assets, pay versus costs, and obligation, you're making way for informed navigation and arranging in the near future. Tomorrow, we'll expand on this establishment by making a customized spending plan and reserve funds procedure that lines up with your monetary objectives.

2

DAY 2: PLANNING AND BUDGETING

Resulting to studying your financial prosperity on Day 1, you by and by have an obvious picture of where you at this point stand. With this getting it, this present time is the ideal open door to move towards proactive financial organization. Day 2 is connected to orchestrating and arranging — critical capacities for making and staying aware of monetary prosperity.

Making a Monetary arrangement That Works for You

Getting a handle on Your Expenses

Before you can make a spending arrangement, you truly need to know where your money is going. Arrange your expenses into two sorts: fixed and variable. Fixed costs are those that remain commonly consistent consistently, for instance, rent or home advance, protection portions, and credit portions. Variable expenses, of course, can waver, similar to food, entertainment, and discretionary spending.

Designating Your Compensation

The way to compelling arranging is tracking down a balance that licenses you to take care of your expenses, save for the future, and participate in your life. A renowned method for apportioning your compensation is the 50/30/20 rule:

half on Needs: These are your essentials, like housing, utilities, and food.

30% on Thinks often about: This order integrates things like eating out, side interests, and other unimportant purchases.

20% on Venture assets and Commitment Repayment: This consolidates building an in the event account, setting something to the side for future goals, and settling commitment.

Saving Frameworks

Paying Yourself First

One of the most mind-blowing saving strategies is to "pay yourself first." This infers zeroing in on hold assets and hypotheses by saving a piece of your compensation when you get it, rather than holding on to see what's left over toward the month's end.

Building a Blustery day account

A hidden bonanza is a basic piece of any money related game plan. Hope to save with the end result of covering 3-6 months of regular expenses. This resource goes probably as a financial support that can keep you above water in a time of shortage without relying upon charge cards or credits.

Targets for Venture reserves

Setting clear, unequivocal goals can help with prodding you to save. Whether it's buying a home, traveling, or making arrangements for retirement, having described targets can help you with staying on target and reach informed decisions about where to administer your hold reserves.

Action Steps

Track Your Spending: For the next month, track every dollar you spend. This will help you with perceiving locales where you can downsize.

Make Your Monetary arrangement: Considering your following, organize your expenses and pay according to the 50/30/20 rule. Change as essential to oblige what is happening.

Do the "Pay Yourself First" Framework: Choose a level of your compensation to normally save or contribute consistently. Set up customized moves to make this cycle reliable.

Start Building Your Hidden bonanza: Open a financial balance unequivocally for your in the event account in case you don't at this point have one. Begin by saving a little, sensible total each check.

Set forth Clear Speculation finances Goals: Record your current second and long stretch money related targets. Check how much money you'll require and by when, then, at that point, process the sum you should save consistently to show up at these goals.

Close to the completion of Day 2, you will have taken basic steps towards organizing your assets. An especially organized enjoying plan not simply helps you with managing your money even more effectively yet furthermore sets the foundation for achieving your financial goals. Remember, the target of arranging isn't to restrict your spending anyway to connect with you to spend unquestionably on what has the greatest effect on you, while at this point getting your money related future.

3

DAY 3: INVESTING FOR THE FUTURE

With a strong financial plan and saving system set up from Day 2, you're currently in a situation to consider how to best develop your abundance through effective money management. Contributing is fundamental for accomplishing independence from the rat race, as it permits your cash to work for you, compounding and expanding in esteem over the long haul.

Prologue to Financial planning

Why Contribute?

The essential objective of financial planning is to develop your abundance over the long haul. On account of the force of accumulated dividends, even little, standard speculations can develop altogether over the long run. Contributing isn't only for the rich; it's a device that anybody can use to get their monetary future.

Grasping Gamble versus Return

All ventures accompany some degree of hazard, and by and large, the expected profit from a speculation is straightforwardly connected with how much gamble it conveys. Higher-risk ventures, similar to stocks, offer the potential for better yields, though lower-risk speculations, similar to securities or investment accounts, offer more unassuming returns yet with less instability.

Kinds of Speculations

Stocks: Possession partakes in an organization that can increment in esteem as the organization develops.

Bonds: Credits you provide for an organization or government, which pay you interest over the long haul.

Shared Assets: Pooled cash from numerous financial backers used to purchase an enhanced arrangement of stocks as well as bonds.

Trade Exchanged Assets (ETFs): Like shared reserves however exchanged on stock trades.

Land: Putting resources into property can turn out revenue through lease and likely appreciation in esteem.

Building Your Speculation Portfolio

Evaluating Your Gamble Resilience

Prior to jumping into effective money management, it's essential to evaluate your gamble resilience —

how much unpredictability in venture esteem you can easily deal with. This will rely upon your monetary objectives, venture timetable, and individual solace with risk.

Broadening

One of the critical techniques in money management is broadening — spreading your ventures across different resource classes to decrease risk. A very much enhanced portfolio can help safeguard against huge misfortunes, as various speculations will respond distinctively to similar monetary occasions.

Beginning Little

You needn't bother with an enormous amount of cash to begin financial planning. Numerous stages permit you to begin with limited quantities and proposition choices for setting up programmed month to month ventures. The key is to begin as soon as could really be expected and contribute reliably.

Activity Steps

Instruct Yourself: Invest energy getting more familiar with various sorts of ventures and how they work. There are many free assets accessible internet, including courses, articles, and recordings.

Decide Your Gamble Resistance: Take a web-based test or talk with a monetary counselor to comprehend your gamble resilience and how it ought to shape your speculation procedure.

Begin Little: Investigate speculation stages that permit you to begin with a limited quantity of cash.

Consider setting up programmed speculations to routinely fabricate the propensity for money management.

Expand: As you begin money management, mean to fabricate a differentiated portfolio that mirrors your gamble resistance and monetary objectives. This could incorporate a blend of stocks, securities, and different ventures.

Survey and Change: Consistently audit your speculation portfolio to guarantee it stays lined up with your monetary objectives and hazard resistance. Be ready to make changes on a case by case basis.

Contributing is a useful asset for creating financial wellbeing, yet moving toward it with an arrangement and a comprehension of the basics is significant. Toward the finish of Day 3, you'll have made significant strides towards coming up with a venture technique that upholds your independence from the rat race objectives.

4

DAY 4: PROTECTING YOUR WEALTH

Placing assets into your future and managing your spending plan are essential stages toward freedom from a futile daily existence, but defending the overflow you assemble is in much the same way as fundamental. Day 4 is given to understanding how to safeguard your money related assets and assurance your overflow is defended for your and your family's future.

Assurance: The Prosperity Net for Your Assets

Kinds of Assurance You Need

Medical care: Shields against financial incidents in light of clinical expenses. Having a methodology that covers your necessities and those of your wards is central.

Additional security: Offers money related help to

your wards if there should arise an occurrence of your problematic end. The ideal extent of consideration depends upon your money related situation and family commitments.

Property and Difficulty Insurance: This consolidates contract holders or occupants assurance and mishap inclusion, shielding against setback or damage to your property and liabilities for any underhandedness you could cause to others.

Reviewing Your Security Needs

Evaluating your security needs is a strong cycle. As your life changing occasions — , for instance, getting hitched, having youths, or buying a house — your insurance essentials will similarly create. Reliably investigating and changing your consideration ensures you're agreeably protected reliably.

Genuine Protection: Safeguarding Your Assets and Decisions

The Meaning of Wills and Inheritance Organizing

A will is a legitimate record that coordinates how your assets should be conveyed after your passing. Without a will, the state closes how your assets are assigned, which most likely won't agree with your longings. Space organizing goes past drafting a will — it consolidates setting up trusts, expecting obligations, and seeking after plans for clinical consideration and money related decisions if you can't make them yourself.

All-encompassing legitimate specialists and Clinical benefits Commands

All-encompassing legitimate power (POA): A definitive report that grants someone you trust the ability to manage your financial issues accepting at least for now that you're incapacitated.

Clinical consideration Order: Generally called a living will, it approaches your cravings for clinical treatment if you can't convey them yourself.

Action Steps

Review Your Insurance Incorporation: Evaluate your continuous assurance policies. Ensure your incorporation resolves your issues and consider invigorating your procedures to reflect any new life changing occasions.

Draft or Update Your Will: In case you don't have a will, the present moment is an optimal chance to make one. In case you at this point have a will, overview it to promise it reflects your continuous wishes and conditions.

Think about Home Readiness: Talk with a money related direction or space orchestrating legal counselor to inspect setting up trusts, charge orchestrating, and various methodology to defend your assets and assurance they are coursed by your cravings.

Spread out a Lawful power and Clinical consideration Order: Sort out who you would trust to go with money related and clinical consideration decisions for the wellbeing of you if you were unable to do in that capacity. Legitimate reports should be prepared to formalize these choices.

Close to the completion of Day 4, you will have tracked down a way tremendous ways of protecting your wealth and assurance your money related wishes are respected, no matter what's not too far off. Shielding your overflow is connected to preparing for the unexpected and guaranteeing that your financial achievements continue to help you and your loved ones, even in trouble.

5

DAY 5: CREATING A SUSTAINABLE WEALTH PLAN

The excursion towards independence from the rat race doesn't end subsequent to evaluating your monetary wellbeing, planning, effective money management, or in any event, setting up assurances for your abundance. A persistent interaction requires ordinary survey and acclimation to line up with your developing life conditions and monetary objectives. Today, you'll figure out how to make an abundance plan that meets your ongoing necessities as well as has the adaptability to adjust to your future self.

Survey and Change Your Monetary Arrangement

Directing Ordinary Surveys

Life is erratic, and your monetary arrangement

ought to be adequately nimble to oblige changes, both in your own life and in the more extensive financial scene. Plan customary surveys of your monetary arrangement — something like one time each year — to evaluate its adequacy and make vital changes.

Adapting to Life Changes

Critical life altering situations, for example, marriage, the introduction of a youngster, a lifelong change, or retirement require a reconsideration of your monetary arrangement. These achievements could influence your pay, costs, protection requirements, and venture methodology. Utilize these minutes as any open doors to adjust your arrangement to your new reality.

Building Propensities for Monetary Achievement

Focus on Constant Learning

The universe of individual accounting and contributing is continuously developing. Remain informed about monetary news, patterns, and instructive assets to arrive at learned conclusions about your riches.

Develop Discipline and Persistence

Growing a substantial financial foundation is a long distance race, not a run. Developing propensities for discipline in saving and effective money management, as well as persistence in seeing your arrangements happen as expected, are vital to accomplishing long haul independence from the rat race.

Setting Up Responsibility Frameworks

Having an emotionally supportive network or

responsibility accomplice can fundamentally build your possibilities adhering to your monetary arrangement. Whether it's a monetary guide, a confided in companion, or a relative, pick somebody who grasps your objectives and can assist with keeping you on target.

Activity Steps

Plan Your Next Audit: Write in your schedule for the following survey of your monetary arrangement. Think about setting updates for other significant monetary undertakings, like taking care of bills or adding to your venture accounts.

Distinguish Regions for Constant Learning: Pick a couple of areas of individual budget or contributing that you need to get familiar with before long. Search for books, courses, or trustworthy monetary news sources to extend your comprehension.

Lay out a Responsibility Framework: Settle on your responsibility accomplice or framework. This could include standard registrations with a monetary counsel or defining monetary objectives with an accomplice or companion.

Observe Your Advancement: Recognize the means you've taken towards independence from the rat race throughout the course of recent days. Commending your advancement can give inspiration and support the significance of your monetary excursion.

By finishing the 5-Day Abundance Plan, you've established the groundwork for your monetary future.

Keep in mind, the arrangement you've made is a living record — it ought to develop and change as you do. Routinely returning to and refining your arrangement will assist you with remaining lined up with your objectives, beat difficulties, and eventually accomplish the independence from the rat race you look for.

CONCLUSION: EMBRACING YOUR FINANCIAL FREEDOM JOURNEY

As we wrap up our 5-day venture towards building a strong starting point for independence from the rat race, it's essential to recognize that this plan isn't the end however the start of a long lasting excursion. Independence from the rat race is definitely not a one-time accomplishment yet a ceaseless course of development, learning, and variation.

The Way You've Set out On

Throughout recent days, you've made huge strides towards understanding and working on your monetary wellbeing. You've surveyed your ongoing monetary circumstance, spread out a financial plan that lines up with your objectives, dove into the universe of money management, and set up measures to safeguard your riches. At long last, you've begun sorting out an economical abundance plan that is customized to your one of a kind monetary circumstance and objectives.

Keeping with it

The way to independence from the rat race is in many cases a long distance race, not a run. It's loaded up with high points and low points, triumphs and mishaps. The following are a couple of key standards to keep you engaged and versatile:

Remain Informed: The universe of money is consistently developing. Keep yourself taught on monetary matters and remain refreshed with market patterns and changes parents in law that might influence your monetary arrangement.

Be Adaptable: Your monetary arrangement is a living record. As your life altering events, so too should your arrangement. Consistently audit and change your spending plan, ventures, and security methodologies to guarantee they stay lined up with your objectives.

Look for Guidance: Make sure to with monetary counsels, charge experts, or lawful specialists. Proficient guidance can be priceless, giving you bits of knowledge and techniques custom fitted to your particular requirements.

The Force of Industriousness

Keep in mind, accomplishing independence from the rat race isn't exclusively about storing up abundance; it's tied in with acquiring the autonomy to live on your conditions. It requires persistence, discipline, and a guarantee to constant improvement. Praise your achievements, regardless of how little, and gain from each insight.

Your Independence from the rat race Outline

"The 5-Day Abundance Plan" has furnished you

with the instruments and information to assume command over your monetary predetermination. However, the most significant component in this plan is you — your activities, choices, and commitment to your monetary prosperity.

Pushing Ahead

As you push ahead, let the standards and procedures you've learned guide your choices. Focus on your objectives, yet additionally partake in the excursion. All things considered, independence from the rat race is as much about the way you travel as the objective you reach.

Last Contemplations

Much obliged to you for leaving on this 5-day excursion to independence from the rat race. Keep in mind, the means you've required for this present week are only the start. Continue to expand on this establishment, remain fixed on your objectives, and constantly take a stab at a superior monetary future. Your way to independence from the rat race is interestingly yours — embrace it, sustain it, and watch it develop.